CHAOS TO FREEDOM

CHAOS TO FREEDOM

Mandeep Kaur Chawla

Worldwide Published by
Pendown Press

PENDOWN PRESS LLP
An ISO 9001 & ISO 14001 Certified Co.,
Regd. Office: 3767A, Kanhaiya Nagar,
Tri Nagar, Delhi-110035
Ph.: 8130886000, 9650072927
E-mail: info@pendownpress.com
Branch Office: 1A/2A, 20, Hari Sadan, Ansari Road,
Daryaganj, New Delhi-110002
Ph.: 011-45794768
Website: PendownPress.com

Edition: 2025

ISBN: 978-93-6338-353-1

Layout and Cover Designed by Pendown Graphics Team
Printed and Bound in India by Thomson Press India Ltd.

Dedication

To all the hardworking operations teams across industries, whose dedication and efforts drive success and growth. May this guide inspire clarity, efficiency, and excellence in every task and project, empowering teams to reach new heights of achievement.

Table of Contents

Acknowledgements

With boundless devotion, I offer my deepest gratitude to Guruji Maharaj, whose divine grace and infinite love have been the guiding light of my journey. Without His sacred will, the very idea of this book would have been beyond my reach.

To my parents, my husband, Dinesh Chawla, and my daughter, Pritika—your steadfast love and support have been my unshakable foundation. Your belief in me has been the wind beneath my wings, and it is through your guidance that this achievement has come to life.

I owe a heartfelt thank you to my mentor, Gaurav Dhameja, whose wisdom and counsel have been a beacon in my journey.

To my mastermind group, MBP - Make People Better, your camaraderie, advice, and relentless encouragement have been my source of strength and growth. This book is as much a testament to your belief in me as it is to my own efforts.

Together, you have all shaped this journey into something extraordinary, and I am forever grateful.

A special thanks to my friend, Dinesh Verma, CEO of Pendown Press, and his team for their continuous support and helpful suggestions throughout this process.

To everyone mentioned here and those who aren't, your contributions have been essential to this journey. Together, we've created something special, and I'm excited to continue growing and succeeding with you all.

Thank you for being a part of this journey.

Preface

"Ever wonder if there's a simpler way to get things done without all the chaos?"

If you've been struggling to keep up with your tasks or feel like things are always slipping through the cracks, you're not alone. We've all been there, juggling too many things at once, wishing for an easier way to manage it all. This book is for anyone who wants to stop wasting time, reduce stress, and get better results with less effort.

Over the years, I've learned a lot about how important it is to streamline operations. Whether you're in real estate, retail, manufacturing, or any other field, the basic idea of making things simpler and more efficient works everywhere.

In this book, I'll share easy-to-follow tips and strategies that have helped me and many others improve the way we work. There's no complicated jargon, just simple advice that you can start using right away to make your life easier and your work more productive.

I believe that things should be simple. Life is already complicated enough, so why make your work harder than it needs to be? By following the steps in this book, you can create smoother systems that not only save you time but also help you get better results.

Let's get started on a journey to simplify your work, improve how you do things, and make your life easier and more successful. I hope this book helps you make the changes you need to work more effectively and see better results in everything you do.

Why Is This Book Different?

This book is different because it's not filled with complicated ideas or long theories that are hard to follow. It's for people who want to see real results, without the confusion. It focuses on simple, practical tips you can use right away, whether you're managing a team, running a business, or just trying to improve your daily work.

Here's what makes this book stand out:

- **Real-Life Examples:** The advice here comes from real situations, not just theory. You'll find examples that make sense in your daily life.

- **Simple and Clear:** I believe in keeping things easy. No hard words, no complicated steps—just simple advice you can follow.

- **Actionable Tips:** It's not just about learning new things; it's about doing them. Each part of the book has steps you can take right away to make things better.

- **Focused on You:** Unlike other books, this one is about helping you with your specific situation. It's not about following a fixed method but about finding what works best for you, your team, and your business.

In short, this book is different because it helps you get real results, without all the extra details. It's for people who want practical advice that works, no matter where you are in your career.

CHAPTER 1

The Tale of "Guru's Handicrafts" and the Power of Operations

"Operational excellence is not just about efficiency, but about creating value at every step."
— Mukesh Ambani, Reliance Industries

Guru, a talented artisan from Jaipur, was known for her beautiful handicrafts. Her small shop was always busy with orders from local customers and tourists. As her fame grew, she decided to expand her business and set up a company, Guru's Handicrafts. Her vision was to take the beauty of Indian craftsmanship to the world.

Initially, Guru managed most of the operations herself—designing products, sourcing materials, managing inventory, and ensuring timely deliveries. However, as the business grew, it became too much for her. Delays started happening, suppliers became unreliable, and customers began complaining. Even though her products were beautiful, Guru's lack of operational expertise started to affect the business.

Recognizing the problem, Guru decided to bring in an Operations Consultant, Mandeep, who had a background in manufacturing and logistics operations. This marked a turning point for Guru's Handicrafts. Here's how the Operations department transformed everything:

Streamlined Supply Chain

One of the biggest challenges Guru faced was sourcing high-quality raw materials consistently. To solve this, Mandeep set up a proper system to evaluate suppliers and built strong relationships with trusted ones. She also created a just-in-time inventory system, which meant they always had the right amount of materials—neither too much nor too little. This system helped avoid waste, reduced unnecessary purchases, and lowered overall costs, keeping the business more efficient and profitable.

Efficient Production Process

Mandeep analyzed the production workflow and noticed that the artisans were spending too much time on tasks that could be simplified. She reorganized the workshop layout, which helped the workers move more easily and save time. She also introduced standardized processes, so everyone knew exactly how to do their jobs. To further improve efficiency, Mandeep trained the artisans to use new tools that sped up their work. As a result, the production process became much faster, and Guru was able to take on larger orders without compromising the quality of her products.

Logistics and Timely Deliveries

Previously, Guru's deliveries were delayed due to poor logistics planning. Mandeep fixed this problem by setting up a reliable courier system, which ensured orders were delivered on time. She also introduced a system to prioritize deliveries based on urgency and location. This made sure that the most important orders were fulfilled first, helping to boost customer satisfaction. Additionally, Mandeep implemented a tracking system that allowed them to monitor deliveries in real-time, giving customers updates and improving the overall delivery experience.

Data-Driven Decision Making

Guru had always made decisions based on intuition. However, Mandeep introduced a new approach based on data. He started tracking everything—from the time it took to complete orders to how happy customers were with the products. With proper reporting and analytics, they were able to spot problems early and anticipate demand trends. This helped the business stay ahead of the competition and make smarter decisions.

Customer Satisfaction

Although Guru's customers loved her craft, delays and occasional quality issues had started to affect her reputation. To address this, Mandeep set up a dedicated customer service team and streamlined the after-sales support, ensuring that any complaints were resolved quickly and efficiently As a result, customer loyalty grew, and repeat orders started coming in.

The Result

With Mandeep leading the Operations department, Guru's Handicrafts flourished. Orders were delivered on time, costs were reduced, and customer satisfaction skyrocketed. Guru could now focus on her true passion—designing and crafting beautiful products—while the Operations department ensured everything behind the scenes ran smoothly.

Conclusion

This story highlights how the Operations department is the backbone of any organization. It transforms vision into reality by ensuring smooth processes, managing resources efficiently, and delivering on customer promises. While creativity and strategy are important, it is operational excellence that keeps an organization running and growing. Without it, even the most innovative ideas can fail.

CHAPTER 2

An Operational Revolution

ABC Builders (Correct name not disclosed due to confidentiality), a rising real estate developer in India, had established a strong reputation for its luxurious residential projects. Their marketing strategies were spot on, and their architects were top-notch. The company had built a brand name synonymous with premium living. However, as the number of projects increased, so did their operational challenges.

Although there was an increasing demand for their properties, the company began facing significant issues. Delays in project completion, cost overruns, and poor coordination between departments started becoming a significant concern. Complaints from homebuyers about delays in possession and incomplete amenities tarnished ABC's reputation.

The Turning Point: Enter the Operations Head

Realizing the growing operational issues, the CEO of ABC Builders hired an experienced Operations Consultant, Mandeep, to manage the complex workings of multiple construction sites, vendor coordination, supply chain, and customer handovers.

Mandeep quickly understood that while the company had been focusing primarily on sales and design, it lacked a strong operational backbone to manage its projects efficiently. Here's how the Operations department turned things around for ABC Builders:

1. **Project Timeline Management**

   One of the major issues was that projects were consistently running behind schedule. The construction teams, suppliers, and contractors weren't well-aligned, causing delays at various stages. Mandeep implemented a comprehensive project management system that tracked every aspect of construction—from land acquisition, material procurement, and contractor timelines, to final handover by using Project management tools.

   By introducing clear milestones and conducting regular progress reviews, the Operations department ensured that every phase of the project was completed on time. This approach improved coordination between the architects, engineers, and construction teams. The same was tracked on the above mentioned tools.

2. **Vendor Management and Cost Control**

   ABC Builders had been facing constant price fluctuations and inconsistent quality of materials. To address this, Mandeep revamped the vendor management system. She focused on building long-term relationships with reliable suppliers and negotiated better deals by committing to larger volume purchases.. He also implemented a supplier rating system to ensure that only high-quality vendors were retained.

   These changes not only improved the quality of materials but also significantly reduced the overall cost of construction.

With Mandeep's operational control over costs, ABC Builders was able to reallocate the savings to improve amenities and speed up project completion, making their properties even more attractive to homebuyers.

3. Efficient Resource Allocation

Previously, labor, machinery, and materials were often underutilized or unevenly distributed across different projects. Mandeep introduced a centralized system to monitor and allocate resources—labor, machinery, and materials—across all sites. This ensured that no site faced delays due to a lack of resources while others were overstaffed.

This system ensured that all construction sites received the resources they needed without overloading any single site. Construction equipment was optimized to reduce idle time, significantly lowering operational costs.

4. Compliance and Legal Coordination

ABC Builders faced delays due to missing permits, environmental clearances, and other legal approvals. Mandeep ensured that the Operations team worked closely with the legal and compliance departments to streamline the approval process, keeping projects in line with regulatory requirements.

This proactive approach helped reduce last-minute delays, fines, and legal battles, ensuring smooth project progression.

5. Customer Handover and Satisfaction

One of the critical areas where ABC was struggling was the final handover of apartments to customers. Issues such as incomplete amenities, unfinished interiors, and inconsistent communication with buyers were damaging the company's reputation.

Mandeep set up a dedicated team within Operations to oversee the final stages of project completion. This team ensured that every unit was inspected for quality, all amenities were completed on time, and buyers were kept informed at every stage. This improved customer satisfaction, reduced complaints, and built trust with homebuyers.

6. **Risk Management and Contingency Planning**

   Real estate development comes with its own set of uncertainties—weather conditions, labor strikes, or unexpected government regulations. Mandeep implemented a risk management strategy, where contingency plans were developed for every possible disruption. By anticipating potential risks, the Operations team could pivot and keep the projects on track.

The Result

Within a year of Mandeep taking charge, ABC Builders saw an incredible turnaround. Projects were completed on or ahead of schedule, costs were controlled, and customer were much happier with the service they received. The company's reputation as a reliable developer was restored, and they could take on more projects without fear of operational failures.

Conclusion

This story illustrates the essential role of the Operations department in the real estate development industry. While marketing, design, and sales are crucial for creating a brand and attracting customers, it's the Operations department that ensures the company delivers on its promises. Efficient project management, cost control, resource allocation, and customer satisfaction all rely on a strong operational framework. Without a well-organized Operations department, even the most ambitious real estate projects can collapse under their complexity.

CHAPTER 3

From Chaos to Control: Ganga Mart's Operational Transformation

---

"In Indian organizations, operational excellence is achieved when technology, people, and processes work in harmony to create a seamless customer experience."
– Sundar Pichai, Google CEO (Indian-origin)

Ganga Mart (Name changed due to Confidentiality), a popular hyperstore chain in India, was expanding quickly with stores in major cities like Delhi, Mumbai, and Bengaluru. It offered a wide range of products, from groceries to electronics, and had built a loyal customer base. However, as the business grew, cracks began to appear in its operations. Customers complained about stockouts, delayed deliveries, and long checkout times. Internally, store employees faced issues with inventory management and communication breakdowns, leading to inefficiency.

The management soon realized that the store's growing size was causing these operational issues, and without fixing them, they couldn't keep up with their expansion or maintain customer satisfaction.

The Problem Before Operations Optimization

Stockouts and Overstocking: Products were either out of stock or overstocked in warehouses. Store managers struggled to predict demand accurately.

➢ **Checkout Delays:** During peak hours, long queues at the billing counter frustrated customers. Cashiers couldn't keep up, which made things worse.

➢ **Miscommunication:** Store managers, suppliers, and inventory teams were not in sync. Orders were often delayed, leading to customer dissatisfaction.

➢ **Employee Disengagement:** Without clear responsibilities and processes, staff were overwhelmed by multiple tasks and struggled to maintain smooth operations.

The management realized that without a well-structured Operations Department, they wouldn't be able to scale effectively or retain their customers in a highly competitive market.

The Turning Point:
Strengthening the Operations Department

To address these issues, Ganga Mart's CEO, Mr. Singh, brought in an experienced Operations Consultant, Mandeep. Her task was to streamline the store's operations across all branches, ensuring consistency, efficiency, and customer satisfaction.

1. **People: Empowering Employees with Clear Roles and Training**

   Ms. Mandeep's first priority was to address the human resource challenge. Employees at Ganga Mart were hardworking, but they lacked training and clear responsibilities, which led to inefficiency and burnout.

➢ **Steps Taken:**

- **Defined Roles:** Mandeep reorganized the workforce, ensuring that each employee had a clearly defined role. Whether it was inventory management, sales floor support, or checkout operations, each team member now knew their specific duties.

- **Training:** She introduced training programs for cashiers, sales staff, and warehouse workers. Cashiers were trained to handle transactions quickly and accurately, while inventory staff were educated on stock management techniques. This significantly improved the workflow.

- **Team Accountability:** Each department was given performance metrics to track their efficiency—inventory accuracy, checkout speed, and customer satisfaction ratings. This sense of ownership motivated employees to take responsibility for their tasks.

➢ **Outcome:** Employee productivity improved, reducing task overlap and inefficiencies. Employees were more confident in their roles, and the overall store atmosphere became more organized.

2. Process: Implementing Standardized Procedures

The next step was to bring consistency to the way all branches worked. Before this, each store had its own way of doing things, causing confusion and delays.

➢ **Steps Taken:**

- **Inventory Management Process:** Ms. Mandeep introduced a centralized inventory management system across all stores. She created a demand forecasting process that analyzed past sales trends, allowing the stores to predict future demand more accurately. This helped reduce both stockouts and overstocking.

- **Replenishment Process:** A daily replenishment process was set up to ensure that products in high demand were reordered on time, preventing empty shelves. Each store was required to submit inventory reports at the end of every day.

- **Checkout Efficiency:** Mandeep introduced a new queuing system during peak hours to reduce long lines. She also implemented a fast-checkout process for customers with fewer items to streamline smaller transactions.

- **Complaint Resolution:** A standardized process for customer complaints was introduced, where issues were logged digitally, assigned to the concerned department, and resolved within a set timeframe. This helped in identifying recurring problems and addressing them proactively.

➢ **Outcome:** Ganga Mart saw a 25% reduction in stockouts and overstocking across all branches. Customer complaints about long queues reduced significantly, and the new processes made employees more efficient in their day-to-day tasks.

3. **Technology: Enhancing Efficiency with Automation and Data**

Ganga Mart's technology was outdated, with stores still relying on manual inventory tracking and disconnected billing systems. Ms. Mandeep understood the store needed better technology to make processes faster, more accurate, and easier to manage.

➢ **Steps Taken:**

- **Point of Sale (POS) Upgrade:** She upgraded the hyperstore's POS system to integrate with the inventory management software. This meant that whenever an item was sold, the inventory would be updated automatically, providing real-time stock levels. This reduced the risk of human error in stock tracking.

- **Barcode System for Stock:** A barcode system was introduced for inventory management. Each product now had a barcode that could be scanned during stocking and checkout, ensuring real-time tracking and reducing the time employees spent managing inventory.

- **Mobile App for Customers:** Mandeep also initiated the development of a mobile app where customers could check product availability, order items for home delivery, and track the status of their orders. This increased customer engagement and provided an additional sales channel.

- **Analytics and Reporting:** Using data analytics tools, the operations department could now analyze foot traffic, peak hours, and customer purchasing patterns. This helped in making informed decisions on staffing and inventory levels.

➢ **Outcome:** The implementation of technology not only reduced manual errors but also made inventory management more efficient. The mobile app became a favorite among customers, making shopping easier and increasing sales. The data tools also helped the store run more smoothly by providing valuable insights into customer behavior.

The Result: Ganga Mart's Operational Transformation

By focusing on **People, Process, Technology and Review Control Mechanism,** Ganga Mart turned its operations around within a year. Here's what they achieved:

➢ **Increased Efficiency:** The new processes and technology reduced operational inefficiencies. Checkout time dropped by 40%, inventory accuracy improved, and overall store performance became more consistent.

➢ **Customer Satisfaction:** With shorter queues, better-stocked shelves, and more responsive customer service, Ganga Mart saw a 20% increase in customer satisfaction scores across its stores.

➢ **Cost Reduction:** The streamlined processes and technology-driven inventory system allowed Ganga Mart to reduce wastage and avoid over-ordering, saving the company a significant amount in operational costs.

➢ **Scalability:** With standardized processes and real-time data, Ganga Mart was now prepared for future growth. They could easily replicate the new model in upcoming stores, ensuring that their expansion would not compromise operational quality.

Conclusion: The Power of the Operations Department

The story of Ganga Mart demonstrates how the **Operations Department** can be the backbone of success in the retail industry. By focusing on aligning **People, Process, Technology, and Review Control Mechanism** Ganga Mart was able to optimize its operations, improve customer satisfaction, and prepare for future expansion.

In a competitive Indian retail landscape, strong operations are what separate businesses that just survive from those that truly thrive. Ganga Mart's journey is a testament to how operational excellence drives both customer loyalty and business growth.

CHAPTER 4

Operations: The Backbone of Business Success

"True operational excellence is not about chasing short-term profits but building sustainable systems that serve both people and the planet."
— Ratan Tata, Tata Group

The Operations Department in an organization can be compared to the spine in human anatomy, which serves as the backbone of the entire body. Just as the spine connects and supports different parts of the body, the operations department connects and supports various functions of a business, ensuring that everything works in harmony.

1. **Spine: Structural Support**

   In the human body, the spine provides structural support, enabling upright posture and facilitating movement. Similarly, the Operations Department provides the framework for the organization, ensuring smooth execution of day-to-day tasks. It helps align various departments such as sales, marketing, finance, and production, allowing them to function seamlessly together.

Without a strong spine, the body would collapse under its own weight. Likewise, without an effective operations team, an organization would struggle with inefficiencies, miscommunication, and chaos.

2. **Nerve Communication: Coordination of Functions**

The spine contains the spinal cord, which is a central hub for transmitting signals between the brain and other parts of the body. The spinal cord ensures that every part of the body receives the right instructions and works in coordination.

The Operations Department plays a similar role in an organization. It acts as the central nervous system, coordinating the flow of information and resources between departments. This ensures that production teams know what to produce, the sales team knows what is available to sell, and customer service can address inquiries based on real-time data. Effective communication and coordination between these departments are crucial for the organization to function properly.

3. **Flexibility and Adaptability: Handling Stress**

The spine is also highly flexible and adaptable, allowing the body to move in different directions and absorb shocks or stresses. This flexibility is critical for adjusting to changing environments or performing complex movements.

Similarly, the Operations Department must be adaptable, flexible, and able to absorb the "shocks" of market changes, supply chain disruptions, or unforeseen challenges. When demand spikes or supply falls short, the operations team needs to pivot quickly, recalibrate processes, and ensure the organization remains functional, just as the spine absorbs physical impact to keep the body moving.

4. Protection: Safeguarding Vital Processes

In human anatomy, the spine protects the spinal cord, which controls most body functions. Any damage to the spine can lead to severe consequences, such as paralysis, because it disrupts the body's ability to function.

Similarly, the Operations Department safeguards the vital processes of an organization. It ensures that the company's resources, such as inventory, labor, and technology, are effectively managed and used in alignment with strategic goals. If operations are poorly managed or neglected, the entire business can suffer—just like how an injury to the spine can halt body movement and disrupt life.

5. Foundation for Growth

Finally, the spine serves as the foundation for growth and development in the human body. It supports the entire skeletal system, enabling physical development and strength as the body grows.

In the same way, the Operations Department serves as the foundation for the growth and scalability of an organization. By implementing efficient processes, optimizing resources, and ensuring smooth operations, it allows the company to grow, take on new projects, expand into new markets, and meet customer demands—much like the spine allows the body to develop and gain strength over time.

Conclusion: Operations as the Backbone

In conclusion, just as the spine is essential to the human body's functionality, the Operations Department is essential to an organization's success. It provides structural support, facilitates coordination, offers flexibility, protects core processes, and serves as the foundation for sustainable growth.

A well-functioning Operations Department ensures keeps the entire organization on track, ready to face challenges and seize new opportunities. Without it, the business risks falling apart— but with it, success is within reach.

CHAPTER 5

A Myth – Operations is difficult

"Success in operations is not about perfection; it's about progress—taking small, incremental steps toward greater efficiency."
– Anand Mahindra, Mahindra Group

Myth: Operations is Difficult

Reality: Operations can seem complex, but with the right approach, it becomes manageable and highly rewarding. Many believe that operations is difficult because it deals with numerous moving parts—people, processes, technology, and review mechanism. However, the perceived difficulty often comes from not having clear systems or the right approach in place.

Here's why operations, though intricate, isn't really as hard as it seems:

1. **Operations is about Process, Not Chaos**

   Myth: Operations is chaotic and unmanageable.

   Reality: Operations is all about creating structured processes and working efficiently. When there are clear standard operating procedures (SOPs) and systems, tasks become repeatable and manageable. What might seem chaotic can actually be streamlined into an organized flow. It's about breaking down complex tasks into smaller, manageable steps.

For example, when Ganga Mart (from our previous story) optimized its inventory management and checkout processes, the once-chaotic experience of stockouts and long queues became smooth and predictable. Operations isn't about chaos but about building **clarity and order.**

2. **Technology Simplifies Operations**

   Myth: Operations requires manual oversight of every little detail.

   Reality: Technology has made it possible to automate many operational processes, from inventory management to customer service. Software solutions, analytics, and AI tools can handle repetitive tasks, provide insights, and even predict future needs. This reduces the burden of manual oversight and allows the operations team to focus on more strategic decisions.

   Using a centralized inventory management system or real-time analytics tools can automate routine processes, making operations more efficient and less hands-on. What used to take hours or days can now be done in minutes with a few clicks.

3. **Operations is About Teamwork, Not a One-Man Show**

   Myth: Operations relies on one person to handle everything.

   Reality: Operations is a team effort. It requires collaboration between different departments—sales, marketing, production, and logistics. The load is shared, not carried by one person. When every team member understands their role, and there's proper communication, operations become smoother and less daunting.

The myth arises because sometimes people think of operations as the sole responsibility of one individual or team. But in reality, the success of operations depends on clear roles, coordination, and collective accountability across the organization.

4. **Flexibility is Key in Operations**

Myth: Operations is rigid and can't adapt quickly to change.

Reality: Operations is about building resilience and flexibility. It involves being prepared for different scenarios and having contingency plans in place. While the processes themselves need to be consistent, they must also be adaptable to changing market conditions, customer demands, or supply chain disruptions.

Good operations management ensures that there are flexible systems in place to adapt quickly without derailing the entire organization. In other words, operations are designed to handle change efficiently, rather than being stuck in rigid routines.

5. **Operations Drives Innovation**

Myth: Operations is just about following routine tasks; it doesn't encourage innovation.

Reality: While operations focus on efficiency, it is also a driver of innovation. By continuously improving processes and exploring new technologies, operations teams can find better ways to reduce costs, improve productivity, and enhance customer satisfaction. Streamlining processes allows organizations to scale and innovate at a faster pace.

In short, operations isn't just a routine task—it's about identifying opportunities for growth and continuous improvement, whether that's through automation, better resource management, or new approaches to customer service.

Conclusion: Operations is Manageable and Essential

The myth that *"operations is difficult"* comes from the misconception that it is a chaotic, all-consuming function. In reality, it is a structured, organized, and collaborative effort designed to make organizations more efficient and agile. With the right tools, processes, and mindset, operations can be both manageable and a critical driver of success. It is not about complexity but about **simplifying, systematizing,** and **optimizing** every aspect of a business for maximum performance.

CHAPTER 6

Let's Learn to Simplify the Process: PPTR Framework

"Operational excellence is when the back office becomes as important as the front office, and every part of the organization works like clockwork."
– Kumar Mangalam Birla, Aditya Birla Group

The **PPTR Framework**—People, Process, Technology, and Review Mechanism—is a a core framework or "thumb rule" for building an efficient and sustainable operations structure. When all four components are in balance, they work together to improve performance and drive growth. Let's break down this framework and see how each component plays a vital role in operations:

1. People: The Heart of Operations

Thumb Rule: Equip and empower people to execute well-defined processes using appropriate technologies.

No operation can succeed without the right people. They are the ones driving every system, executing tasks, and bringing creativity and adaptability to the workplace.

- **Hiring and Training:** Having skilled employees with the right competencies is crucial for the smooth execution of tasks. Ensuring they are well-trained and empowered with proper knowledge boosts efficiency.

- **Collaboration and Communication:** Effective collaboration between teams such as production, logistics, and customer service is essential for streamlined operations.

- **Leadership and Culture:** The leadership team must instill a culture of continuous improvement, operational excellence, and adaptability to change.

Example: In an Indian retail hyperstore, the operations team ensures that staff members at checkout counters are well-trained to use billing software, manage customer queries, and handle inventory systems efficiently.

2. **Process: The Blueprint for Efficiency**

Thumb Rule: Standardize and optimize processes to ensure efficiency, consistency, and scalability.

A clear, well-defined process is the foundation of smooth operations. Without documented workflows and operating procedures, even the most talented people and advanced technologies can fail to deliver.

- **Standard Operating Procedures (SOPs):** Processes must be documented and standardized across the organization. SOPs provide employees with clear guidelines on how to carry out tasks efficiently.

- **Continuous Improvement:** Processes should never remain static. Operations teams should regularly review and refine processes to eliminate waste, reduce bottlenecks, and improve turnaround times.

- **Adaptability:** While standardization is important, processes should be flexible enough to adapt to changes in market conditions, technology, or customer preferences.

Example: In a large hyperstore, standardized inventory management processes help ensure that products are stocked efficiently and displayed properly. Clear procedures for ordering and stocking reduce errors and prevent stockouts or overstock situations.

3. **Technology: The Catalyst for Speed and Scalability**

Thumb Rule: Leverage technology to automate processes, enhance accuracy, and scale operations efficiently.

Technology is the enabler that boosts both people and processes. It allows for greater efficiency, improved accuracy, and enhanced scalability.

- **Automation:** Implementing automation tools can significantly reduce human error, free up manpower, and speed up operations. From inventory management systems to customer relationship management (CRM) software, technology simplifies tasks.

- **Data and Analytics:** Real-time data helps in making informed decisions. Analytics can track key metrics such as lead times, customer satisfaction, inventory levels, and financial performance.

- **Scalability:** As organizations grow, technology allows processes to scale effectively. For example, cloud-based systems enable organizations to handle larger volumes of transactions without a proportionate increase in costs.

Example: An advanced POS (point-of-sale) system in a hyperstore helps manage billing, tracks customer purchases, and updates the inventory system in real time. This ensures efficiency at the counter while preventing manual errors.

4. **Integrating a Review Control Mechanism**

The Review Control Mechanism adds discipline to the operational environment and fosters a culture of excellence by constantly monitoring, analyzing, and refining all the other components (People, Process, and Technology).

Key Benefits of the Review Control Mechanism:

1. **Agility and Adaptability:** With constant monitoring and feedback, organizations can quickly adapt to changes and challenges, keeping their operations nimble and responsive.

2. **Risk Mitigation:** Regular reviews help in identifying potential risks, allowing organizations to proactively take corrective action rather than responding reactively to crises.

3. **Efficiency and Optimization:** By continuously evaluating processes and technology, inefficiencies are identified and addressed, resulting in streamlined operations and reduced costs.

4. **Improved Employee Performance:** With performance monitoring and feedback, the organization can support employees with targeted training, addressing skill gaps and improving productivity.

5. **Data-Driven Decisions:** The review mechanism provides valuable data and insights, enabling leaders to make informed decisions based on real performance metrics.

How the Review Control Mechanism Complements PPT

- ➤ **People:** Ensures ongoing performance management, training, and engagement, allowing for the continuous development of human capital.

- ➤ **Process:** Identifies areas for process improvements and ensures that workflows are optimized, effective, and compliant with standards.

- ➤ **Technology:** Evaluates technology effectiveness, ensuring that tools and platforms remain up-to-date, well-utilized, and aligned with organizational needs.

- ➤ **Example:** Application in a Subscription Model Organization

In a subscription-based organization, the Review Control Mechanism would regularly assess the following:

- ➤ **People:** Evaluate the sales team's performance in customer acquisition and retention. Provide feedback and targeted training where necessary.

- ➤ **Process:** Monitor the customer onboarding and subscription renewal processes for efficiency and customer satisfaction.

- ➤ **Technology:** Ensure that the CRM and subscription management platforms are functioning optimally and providing accurate data.

- ➤ **Review:** Implement periodic reviews of customer churn rates, feedback from customer support teams, and technology performance to ensure continuous growth and improvement.

Thumb Rule for Operations Success

The key to effective operations lies in balancing the four elements of the **PPTR Framework.** If any one of these components is underdeveloped or overemphasized, operational efficiency can suffer. Here's how each component interacts:

1. **People without Processes:** Even the best people can't function effectively without clear guidance. The lack of standard processes can lead to inconsistencies, delays, and errors.

2. **Processes without People:** The most optimized processes still need talented people to execute them. Without proper staffing, even the most well-documented SOPs will fail.

3. **Technology without Process or People:** The most advanced technology is useless if processes aren't defined and people aren't trained to use it.

4. All three components People, Process and Technology will fail if proper RCM - Review Control Mechanism is not implemented.

Conclusion

The **PPTR framework of People, Process, Technology and RCM is the thumb rule of operations.** By balancing these four critical components, organizations can optimize efficiency, reduce operational costs, improve customer satisfaction, and scale for growth. People drive the operations, processes provide the structure, and technology serves as the enabler—each reinforcing the other to create a strong operational backbone for any organization. When all these elements work together, they form a seamless and resilient system, ensuring long-term success and continuous improvement in any organization.

CHAPTER 7

Building Success: Applying the PPTR Framework to Real Estate Development

---

"In Indian businesses, operational excellence means weaving innovation into the core of operations and making every process smarter."
— Vineet Nayar, HCL Technologies

In a real estate developer organization, the PPTR framework of People, Process, Technology and RCM is crucial for ensuring efficient operations. Let's apply this rule to see how each element plays a vital role in driving the success of real estate projects, from land acquisition to construction and sales.

1. People: The Expertise Behind Every Project

Thumb Rule: Empower skilled individuals at every stage of the development process with clear roles and collaboration.

People are at the heart of real estate development, where diverse expertise is required for various tasks such as land acquisition, design, construction, legal compliance, sales, and marketing. A well-coordinated team is essential for success.

- **Project Managers:** They oversee all phases of the project, from planning to execution, ensuring timelines are met and budgets are maintained.

- **Architects and Engineers:** These specialists bring technical expertise to ensure buildings meet safety standards and are aesthetically designed.

- **Sales and Marketing Teams:** Responsible for selling the developed properties, these teams need to have a clear understanding of customer needs and market trends.

- **Site Workers and Contractors:** Skilled workers on-site need to be properly trained and supervised to ensure construction is carried out according to plan.

Example: A well-coordinated sales team ensures potential buyers are provided with accurate information, while the construction team makes sure the properties are completed on time, minimizing delays.

2. **Process: The Blueprint for Every Stage**

Thumb Rule: Standardize and streamline the real estate development lifecycle to reduce delays, errors, and rework.

Real estate development is a complex, multi-stage process that involves various stakeholders. Having well-defined processes is critical to ensure that projects are delivered on time, within budget, and to the required quality.

- **Land Acquisition Process:** Clear guidelines for identifying, negotiating, and acquiring land are essential. This reduces the time and legal risks associated with land deals.

- **Construction SOPs:** Establishing standard operating procedures (SOPs) for construction activities helps maintain quality and safety standards, and ensures efficient resource utilization.

- **Sales and Handover Process:** From generating leads to closing deals and handling customer queries, the sales process needs to be systematic to prevent any drop in communication. The handover process must also be well-defined for seamless customer experience.

- **Budget and Cost Control:** Processes for budget estimation, financial reporting, and cost control ensure that resources are allocated efficiently, and any deviations are tracked and rectified early on.

Example: A well-documented construction process ensures that each stage, from the foundation to electrical, plumbing, and finishing, is completed according to plan, avoiding delays and costly rework.

3. **Technology: The Enabler for Growth and Efficiency**

Thumb Rule: Leverage technology to automate tasks, improve decision-making, and enhance project visibility across all stages.

In real estate development, technology acts as a catalyst for efficiency by improving coordination between departments, automating repetitive tasks, and providing real-time data for better decision-making.

- **Construction Management Software:** Tools such as project management platforms help track project progress, manage resources, and flag delays in real-time.

- **BIM (Building Information Modeling):** BIM technology allows architects, engineers, and contractors to collaborate on a single 3D model, reducing errors and improving construction efficiency.

- **CRM Systems for Sales:** Real-time tracking of leads, customer interactions, and sales pipelines through a CRM system allows the sales team to be more organized and responsive.

- **Analytics and Reporting Tools:** Technology can provide detailed reports on costs, timelines, and market trends, helping management make informed decisions about new projects and existing ones.

Example: A real estate company uses a centralized platform that integrates construction progress with financial updates. This allows project managers to track whether each stage is on budget and on time, and sales teams to check inventory status instantly.

Applying the PPTR Framework to Real Estate Operations

To apply the **PPTR Framework of People, Process, Technology and RCM** in real estate development:

1. **People:** Ensure the right mix of expertise in project management, construction, legal compliance, sales, and marketing, with strong interdepartmental communication. Every team member must know their role and work together seamlessly.

2. **Process:** Develop standardized procedures for land acquisition, design approvals, construction workflows, financial tracking, and sales. SOPs should be in place for each

department to minimize delays, avoid rework, and enhance overall efficiency.

3. **Technology:** Implement cutting-edge tools like project management software, CRM systems, and analytics to streamline operations and provide real-time insights. Use automation to reduce manual work, allowing the team to focus on more strategic tasks.

4. **RCM:** In a Real Estate Developer Organization, the Review Control Mechanism (RCM) is essential for maintaining high standards in managing people, optimizing processes, and leveraging technology across complex projects. Implementing RCM ensures continuous improvement, risk mitigation, and alignment with organizational goals.

Conclusion: The Backbone of Real Estate Operations

In the real estate sector, balancing People, Process, Technology, and RCM is key to smooth operations. People provide the expertise, processes bring order and consistency, and technology ensures efficiency and scalability. A real estate developer that manages this balance well can deliver projects on time, within budget, and with the highest level of quality, ensuring long-term success and customer satisfaction.

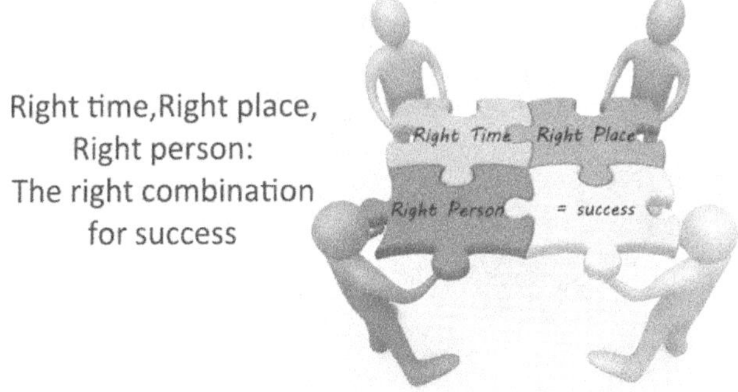

Every Output of any Process in the organization must be an Input to other process

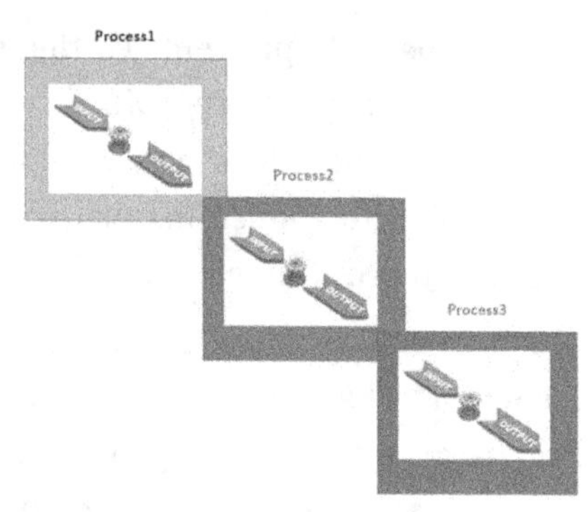

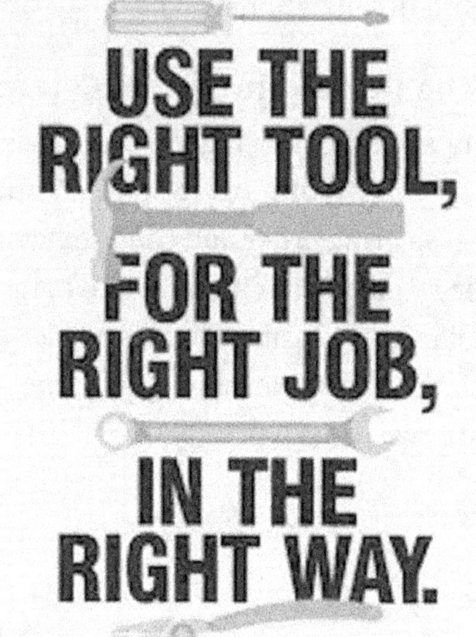

Safeguarding the Organization from Within

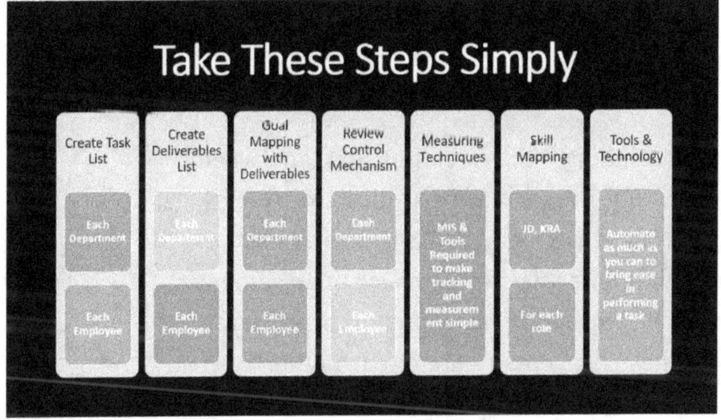

OOOO

CHAPTER 8

Goals, KPI, KRA, Tasks Are Not Scary Words

"Achieving operational excellence in India requires not just technology, but a deep understanding of local markets, people, and cultural nuances."
– Adi Godrej, Godrej Group

Understanding the relationship between **Goals, Key Performance Indicators (KPIs), Key Result Areas (KRAs),** and **Tasks** is crucial for effective performance management and achieving goals in any organization. Here's how these concepts relate to each other:

Representation of Relationships

Explanation of Each Component

1. Goals: The Big Picture

- **Definition:** Goals are broad, high-level objectives that an organization aims to achieve. They set the direction and vision for the organization.

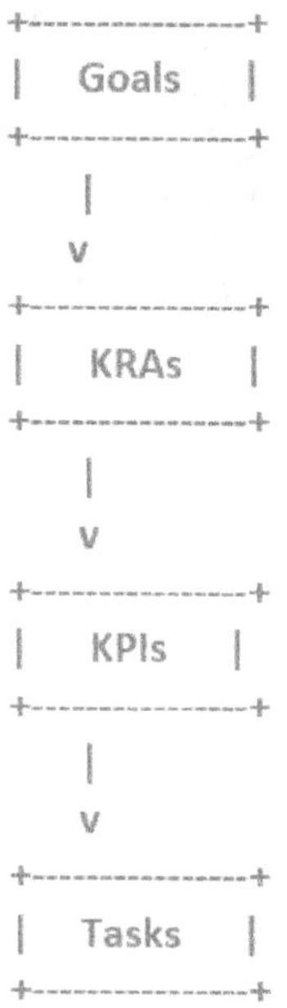

- **Example:** "Increase market share in the real estate sector by 15% in the next fiscal year."

2. **Key Result Areas (KRAs): The Focus Points**

   - **Definition:** KRAs are specific areas or domains where results are expected to be achieved to meet the overall goals. They define the key focus areas that contribute to the goals.

   - **Example:** For the goal of increasing market share, the KRAs might include:
     - Sales Performance
     - Customer Satisfaction
     - Marketing Effectiveness

3. **Key Performance Indicators (KPIs): The Measurable Metrics**

   - **Definition:** KPIs are specific, measurable values that indicate how effectively an individual or organization is achieving key objectives. They provide a way to evaluate success in achieving the KRAs.

   - **Example:** KPIs for the KRA of Sales Performance might include:
     - Number of units sold
     - Revenue generated
     - Conversion rate of leads to sales

4. **Tasks: The Action Steps**

   - **Definition:** Tasks are the specific activities or actions that individuals or teams need to complete to achieve the

KPIs. They are the "to-dos" that drive progress toward KRAs and ultimately the goals.

- **Example:** Tasks for the KPI of "Number of units sold" might include:
  - Conducting market research
  - Developing targeted marketing campaigns
  - Training the sales team on new strategies

Summary of Relationships

➢ **Goals** set the direction and define what the organization wants to achieve.

➢ **KRAs** break down these goals into specific areas that need focus to achieve the overall objectives.

➢ **KPIs** provide measurable indicators that allow tracking of progress towards each KRA.

➢ **Tasks** are the concrete actions that teams or individuals undertake to achieve the KPIs.

By clearly defining these relationships, organizations can align their teams towards common objectives, monitor performance, and ensure that everyone understands their roles in achieving the larger goals.

○○○○

CHAPTER 9

Let's Understand the RACI Matrix

A **RACI** matrix is a simple and powerful tool used in project management to clarify roles and responsibilities within a team. The acronym RACI stands for:

- **R: Responsible** – The person(s) who actually performs the task or activity.

- **A: Accountable** – The person who is ultimately answerable for the task or decision being made. They ensure it is completed correctly.

- **C: Consulted** – People who provide information, advice, or input before the task is performed or the decision is made.

- **I: Informed** – People who are kept in the loop about the task or decision after it is made or completed.

Breakdown of RACI Elements

1. **Responsible (R):**

   - The person(s) directly doing the work. They are responsible for completing the task or project.

- This is the action-oriented role.

- There can be multiple people responsible for a task.

- Example: In a real estate development project, the construction manager is responsible for overseeing the physical building of the project.

2. **Accountable (A):**

   - The person ultimately accountable for the task or project.

   - This is the person who ensures the task is completed satisfactorily and is usually the one who reviews or approves the work.

   - There can be only one accountable person per task, to avoid confusion.

   - Example: The project director is accountable for the entire real estate project, ensuring that it is delivered on time and within budget.

3. **Consulted (C):**

   - People whose opinions, advice, or expertise are sought before making decisions or performing tasks.

   - They contribute valuable insights but are not responsible for carrying out the work or making final decisions.

   - Example: The legal team may be consulted to ensure that all regulations are being followed for land acquisition or permits.

4. **Informed (I):**

   - People who are kept informed about progress or decisions, but do not contribute directly to the task.

- They are usually updated on outcomes, so they stay aligned with the project's status.

- Example: The finance team may be informed about the completion of key project milestones to manage financial planning.

Benefits of the RACI Model

➢ **Clarity:** It clarifies who is responsible, accountable, consulted, and informed for every task or decision. This reduces confusion.

➢ **Avoiding Overlap:** It ensures that there is only one person accountable, avoiding potential conflicts or gaps in responsibility.

➢ **Effective Communication:** By clearly defining who should be consulted and informed, communication flows more smoothly across teams.

➢ **Project Efficiency:** The model reduces delays by clearly identifying who is needed at each step, preventing unnecessary back-and-forth.

Example of a RACI Matrix for a Real Estate Developer Project

Task	Responsible	Accountable	Consulted	Informed
Land Acquisition	Acquisition Manager	Project Director	Legal Team	Finance Team
Construction Planning	Construction Manager	Project Director	Architects, Engineers	Sales Team
Marketing Strategy	Marketing Team	Marketing Director	Branding Agency	Sales Team

Sales and Client Management	Sales Team	Sales Director	Marketing Team, Legal Team	Finance Team
Project Completion Approval	Construction Manager	Project Director	Architects, Legal Team	All Departments

How to Build a RACI Matrix

1. **Identify Tasks:** List all the tasks or activities involved in the project.

2. **Identify Roles:** List all the roles or people involved in the project.

3. **Assign RACI:** For each task, assign one or more people or roles under R (Responsible), A (Accountable), C (Consulted), and I (Informed).

4. **Review and Communicate:** Ensure that the matrix is clear, has no overlaps, and is communicated effectively across the team.

Conclusion

The RACI Matrix is an effective tool for managing roles and responsibilities in any organization, particularly in complex projects like real estate development. It ensures accountability, avoids confusion, and helps streamline communication, making operations more efficient. By clearly defining who is responsible, accountable, consulted, and informed, organizations can enhance productivity, teamwork, and project success.

CHAPTER 10

Benefits of Streamlining the Operations Department

Streamlining the operations department can yield numerous benefits across various industries. Here's a list of key advantages:

1. **Increased Efficiency**

   - **Optimized Processes:** Streamlining operations leads to more efficient workflows, reducing bottlenecks and minimizing delays.

   - **Faster Decision-Making:** Clear processes enable quicker decision-making and responsiveness to changes.

2. **Cost Savings**

   - **Reduced Operational Costs:** Cuts down on overhead expenses, freeing up resources for growth initiatives.

   - **Minimized Waste:** Streamlined processes reduce waste in materials, time, and resources.

3. **Enhanced Quality**

   - **Consistent Standards:** Streamlined operations help maintain high-quality standards and reduce defects or errors.

- **Improved Customer Satisfaction:** Better quality leads to higher customer satisfaction, fostering loyalty and repeat business.

4. **Scalability**

- **Easier Growth Management:** Streamlined operations provide a scalable framework that can easily accommodate growth, whether through new products, services, or markets.

- **Flexible Systems:** Adaptable processes can be quickly modified to meet changing demands.

5. **Better Resource Utilization**

- **Optimal Allocation:** Resources (human, financial, or material) are allocated more effectively, maximizing productivity.

- **Reduced Idle Time:** Employees spend less time on unnecessary tasks and more on value-added activities.

6. **Improved Communication and Collaboration**

- **Clear Roles and Responsibilities:** Streamlined processes clarify roles, reducing confusion and enhancing teamwork.

- **Enhanced Cross-Departmental Coordination:** Better communication channels improve collaboration between different departments.

7. **Data-Driven Insights**

- **Real-Time Analytics:** Streamlined operations often involve systems that provide real-time data and analytics for informed decision-making.

- **Performance Measurement:** Easier tracking of key performance indicators (KPIs) helps identify areas for improvement.

8. Risk Management

- **Proactive Issue Identification:** Streamlined processes facilitate early detection of potential risks or problems, allowing for proactive management.

- **Compliance Assurance:** Standardized operations help ensure adherence to regulations and industry standards, reducing legal risks.

9. Enhanced Customer Experience

- **Timely Delivery:** Streamlined operations improve the speed and reliability of service or product delivery, enhancing customer experience.

- **Personalized Service:** Efficient systems allow for more personalized customer interactions, improving engagement and satisfaction.

10. Focus on Core Competencies

- **Delegation of Operational Tasks:** A streamlined operations department allows leadership to delegate routine tasks, enabling them to focus on strategic planning and business development.

- **Innovation Opportunities:** With operational efficiencies, teams can dedicate more time to innovation and exploring new business opportunities.

11. Employee Satisfaction

- **Reduced Stress:** Clear and efficient processes minimize confusion and workload stress for employees, leading to higher job satisfaction.

- **Career Development:** Employees can focus on skill development and growth opportunities rather than getting bogged down by inefficiencies.

12. Competitive Advantage

- **Market Responsiveness:** Streamlined operations enable quicker adaptations to market changes, keeping the organization competitive.

- **Brand Reputation:** Consistent quality and reliable service enhance brand reputation, attracting more customers.

Conclusion

In summary, streamlining the operations department can significantly enhance an organization's performance across various dimensions. By improving efficiency, reducing costs, and fostering a culture of quality and innovation, businesses can position themselves for sustainable growth and competitive advantage in their respective industries.

OOOO

CHAPTER 11

Dashboard Example for a Real Estate Developer: Operations Team

A well-structured dashboard provides a comprehensive view of ongoing projects, resources, finances, and risks, enabling efficient management and strategic decision-making. Below is a detailed example of a dashboard for the Operations Department:

Dashboard Structure for Operations Department

1. **Overview Section**

   - **Total Projects in Progress:** Number of ongoing projects.

   - **Completed Projects:** Number of projects completed within the last quarter.

   - **Upcoming Projects:** List of projects scheduled to start in the next quarter.

2. **Project Status Tracking**

   - **Project Timeline:**

     - Gantt chart showing project timelines, key milestones, and completion percentages.

   - **Current Phase of Projects:** Breakdown of projects by phases (Planning, Construction, Finalization, etc.).

- **On-Schedule vs. Delayed Projects:** Percentage of projects on track vs. delayed.

3. **Financial Metrics**

   - **Budget Utilization:** Percentage of the budget used vs. remaining for each project.

   - **Cost Variance:** Show discrepancies between the budgeted and actual costs.

   - **Revenue Forecast:** Expected revenue from ongoing projects, segmented by project.

4. **Resource Management**

   - **Resource Allocation:** Overview of workforce allocation across projects (e.g., architects, engineers, contractors).

   - **Utilization Rate:** Percentage of workforce effectively utilized.

   - **Vendor Performance:** Ratings of vendors based on timely delivery, quality of work, and cost-effectiveness.

5. **Quality and Compliance**

   - **Quality Assurance Metrics:** Number of quality checks performed, issues detected, and resolved.

   - **Compliance Status:** Overview of compliance with local regulations, permits, and safety standards.

   - **Client Feedback Scores:** Ratings and feedback from clients regarding completed projects.

6. **Risk Management**

   - **Identified Risks:** List of potential risks (e.g., financial, operational, environmental) associated with current projects.

- **Mitigation Strategies:** Brief descriptions of strategies in place to manage identified risks.
- **Incident Reports:** Number of incidents reported and status of resolution.

7. **Key Performance Indicators (KPIs)**

- **Average Project Completion Time:** Tracks the average duration from project initiation to completion.
- **Customer Satisfaction Rate:** Percentage of customers satisfied with project outcomes.
- **Employee Satisfaction Rate:** Employee feedback on workplace environment and operations.

8. **Action Items and Alerts**

- **Upcoming Deadlines:** Alerts for critical deadlines approaching (e.g., permits due, inspections).
- **Key Decisions Needed:** Highlight decisions that require the owner's attention.
- **Performance Alerts:** Notifications for any significant deviations from KPIs or project timelines.

9. **Visualizations**

- **Charts and Graphs:** Use pie charts, bar graphs, and line charts for easy visual interpretation of data.
- **Heat Maps:** Show areas of concern in project timelines, budget overruns, or resource allocation.

Benefits of the Dashboard

➢ **Quick Insights:** Provides a quick, at-a-glance overview of operations, allowing the business owner to stay informed without diving into details.

- ➤ **Data-Driven Decisions:** Enables informed decision-making based on real-time data and trends.

- ➤ **Focus on Strategy:** Frees up time for the owner to focus on sales, marketing, and strategic growth initiatives.

- ➤ **Proactive Management:** Helps in identifying potential issues early and addressing them proactively.

- ➤ **Enhanced Accountability:** Facilitates accountability by clearly displaying KPIs and performance metrics.

By implementing a dashboard like this, the business owner can maintain oversight of operations while dedicating more time to strategic activities, ultimately driving growth and success for the real estate development business.

OOOO

Let's Make It Happen

Now, you have two options:

1. **Go Solo with the Insights** – Take the strategies, tips, and lessons shared in this book and put them into action. Start improving your operations and see the results for yourself.

2. **Have me by your side** – If you want a more hands-on approach and personalized guidance, I'm here to help you every step of the way. Together, we can fine-tune the strategies to match your unique needs and make sure you're on the path to success.

The choice is yours, but I'm ready to help you no matter which path you choose. Want to connect with me directly? Send me an email at **mandeep@namahconsultants.com** to schedule a one-on-one meeting.

Let's make your next chapter a success!